The Fool's

His journey through the tarot by poetry

Poetry by Christopher Cairns

None of the poetry in this book may be reproduced in any form without the permission in writing of the author.

Images in this book are from the Rider-Waite tarot deck. Arthur Edward Waite was the author and copyright holder who died in 1942.

ISBN: 978-0-244-86878-9

About this book

I have been reading Tarot for many years. At the same time, I love to write poetry in my spare time. I've no pretensions of being a great poet, its just something I love to do.

I hope that by telling the Fool's journey through poetry this will help those who are learning or teaching tarot through the simple story I tell. Christopher Cairns

Contents

Page

1	The Fool's journey through the Major Arcana
25	The Fool's Journey with Pentacles
37	The Fool's Journey with Swords
49	The Fool's Journey with Wands
61	The Fool's Journey with Cups
73	The Fool's Journey through the Court Cards
75	The Fool and the Royal House of Cups
81	The Fool and the Royal House of Swords
87	The Fool and the Royal House of Pentacles
93	The Fool and the Royal House of Wands.
99	The Fool's Journey End

The Fool's Journey through the Major Arcana

There is nothing like a Fool they say
Someone clueless he can be
No experience of anything
And sets out to journey free

THE FOOL.

He reaches a Magician
He's taught all he can achieve
He can manifest anything he wants
He just has to believe

The High Priestess then teaches him
There is more than he can see
There is a mystery deeply so profound
There is more in the world than he

The Fool then meets the Empress
Who nourishes him like a mother
Shows him all nature's loveliness
And all the love for one another

The Fool then meets the Emperor
To learn of structure law and rule
He knows this is another stage
To become less of a Fool

The Hierophant then teaches him
How to think behave believe
And now the Fool is growing fast
Soon his childhood he will leave

He sees two people up ahead
Lovers, an Angel up above
He can now make choices for himself
And if he chooses fall in love

A Chariot then pulls along side
And he boards with little fear
And he learns control with firm of hand
Towards his future he must steer

In doing this he learns a Strength
A lion's heart but in the mind
That fighting is not the only way
You can defeat by being kind

He comes across a Hermit
Standing quietly by a stone
And from him learns some lessons
You must learn by being alone

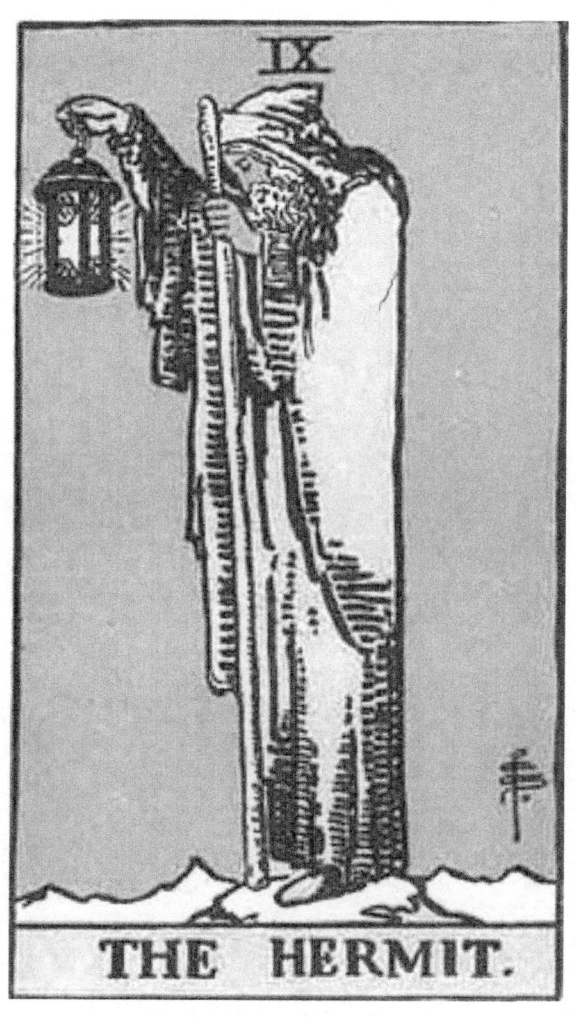

A wheel comes off his chariot
And he crashes with a frown
This is the Wheel of Fortune law
Life can be up but can be down

He accepts the then next lesson
Justice surely comes along
There will always be a price to pay
Do you good or do you wrong

Then walking on the road again
He sees the Hanged Man upside down
With a radiant light around his head
Like a shiny peaceful crown

Aghast he sees Death up ahead
He shakes with mortal fear
But Death say's worry not dear Fool
Each end of life new life is here

The Fool he then met Temperance
And is taught to look and see
Do every thing in balance
And he will live in harmony

But the Devil suddenly appears
Do not listen to him Fool
Why not look at your wicked side
It really is so cool

Within his mind a Tower explodes
It was time for reevaluation
With destruction of a way of thought
There is a chance of more creation

He sees the Star shine brightly
And it's really only then
He is filled with heavenly hope and faith
Seeing light there once again

But in the Moon he is reminded
Not all is as it seems
Subconscious shadows fears remain
Like a fitful night of dreams

THE MOON.

But come the morning is the Sun
With radiant energy glows
Shows all abundance life and joy
Yes he is blessed he knows

This is his day of Judgement
He is reborn and travelled well
He has grown now in so many ways
With so many tales to tell

JUDGEMENT.

He sees the World then up ahead
He is a Fool no longer then
He has completed now the journey
But he sets back out again

The Fool's Journey with Pentacles

Another journey beckons
He sees another magic hand
Bearing a pentacle that represents
All things material in this land

The Ace is a beginning
One pentacle here to start
Opportunity career excitement
And abundance in his heart

He comes across a juggler
Two pentacles moving free
He learns to manage many things
To live a balanced life like he

He enters a new cathedral
Men gather in admiration
This three of pentacles teaches him
The lesson of collaboration

Along the road he sees a man
Four pentacles held so tight
As if scarcity would come along
And steal away at night

A nearby church five pentacles shine
Bright in the stained glass window
Two beggars pass not noticing
Showing somewhere warm to go

A gentle man six pentacles
Was standing in the square
Sharing what he could afford
To the not so well off there

Along the road he sees a farmer
Bush, seven pentacles all aglow
It tells the Fool to see long term
Plant seeds and they will grow

He meets a man eight pentacles
Worked with precision care and will
He learns it takes hard work and toil
To be a master of your skill

In a garden stands a lady
With a falcon on her hand
Nine pentacles scattered all around
Showing abundance here so grand

In a village square, ten pentacles
Show happy family love and song
Show abundance in all earthy things
Now this Fool must travel on

The Fool's Journey with Swords

Now the Fool must journey on
His life is never bored
Another magic hand appears
And offers him a sword

Ace of swords is a beginning
Air represents this shiny tool
Conflict change or power
Be it good or used to rule

He encounters then a woman
Sitting blindfold on a stool
Two swords show indecision
And thinks I'm not the only Fool

Three of swords show heart is broken
And there is a stormy cloud above
It teaches him there's pain in life
Where ever there is love

Four of swords show knight a sleeping
He sees the knight must rest tonight
To be ready for the morrows war
Another battle he must fight

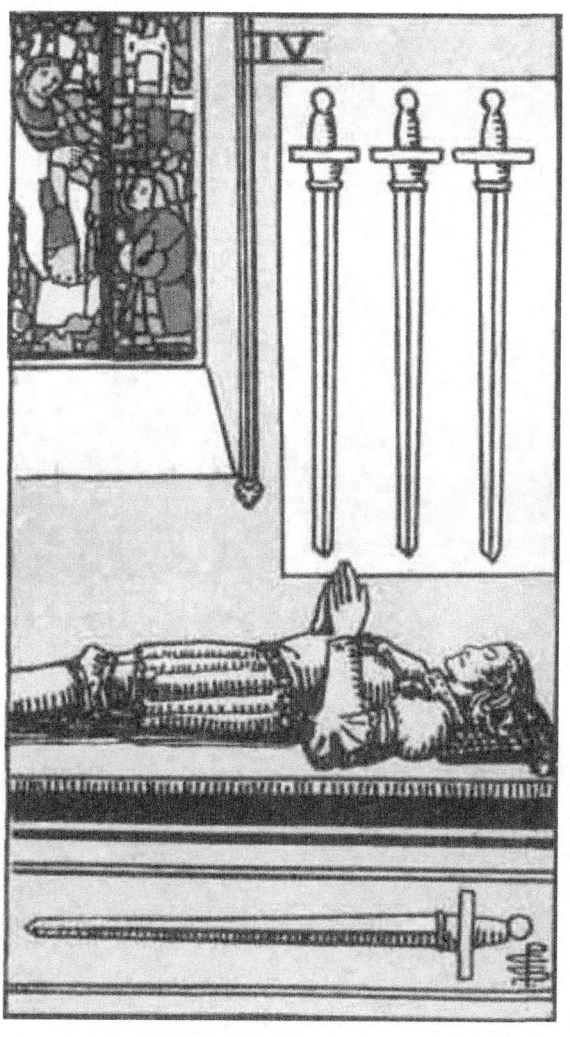

There is a sly looking man collecting
Five swords, the prize for he
The lesson is there must be grace
If you win a victory

The Fool comes across a river
Two sad people sail across
Six swords that laden down the boat
To signify their loss

On the banks he sees a scoundrel
Seven swords there in his hands
He knows he sees a thief at work
And now betrayal understands

The eight swords sees the lady
Still blindfolded he can see
Her negative thoughts so self imposed
Will never allow her to be free

He stops the night in a cosy inn
But sleep will not be kind
Nine swords of worry all above
Go racing through his mind

Ten of swords is now complete
He has suffered all that's gone before
The Fool now understands all this
And now the Fool must journey more

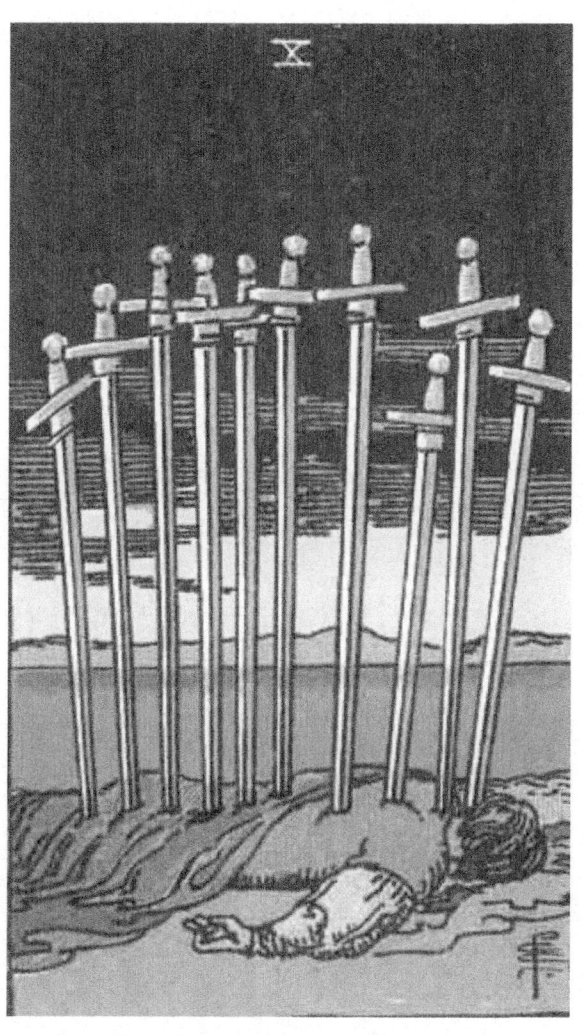

The Fool's Journey with Wands

The Fool has journeyed far and wide
But now must journey more
To learn and quest in minor ways
And learn more than before

Looks to the sky and sees a wand
Held by a magic hand
His eyes so wide at such a sight
And tries to understand

The Ace of Wands does offer
Inspiration growth and fire
New ideas potential excitement new
These things he does desire

He journeys further up the road
A man two wands in hand
Tells him develop ideas anew
Plan think and understand

He meets a man with wands a three
An idea is now in motion
Work is now set out to be
Being real with fire emotion

Foundation built and now he can
Relax with his friends around
Happiness and harmony here
It is a joyful place he's found

He sees five boys there fighting
Their wands waving in the breeze
In playful jest shows conflict
A need for harmony here he sees

The boys all start a cheering
As a man comes riding by
With a wand held high to show success
Now six wands wave cheering high

Now further on his journey
He sees a man upon a hill
Seven wands show he is fighting
He perseveres with all his will

Eight wands come flying through the air
Movement fast at rapid pace
He knows now he must journey more
And leave this learning place

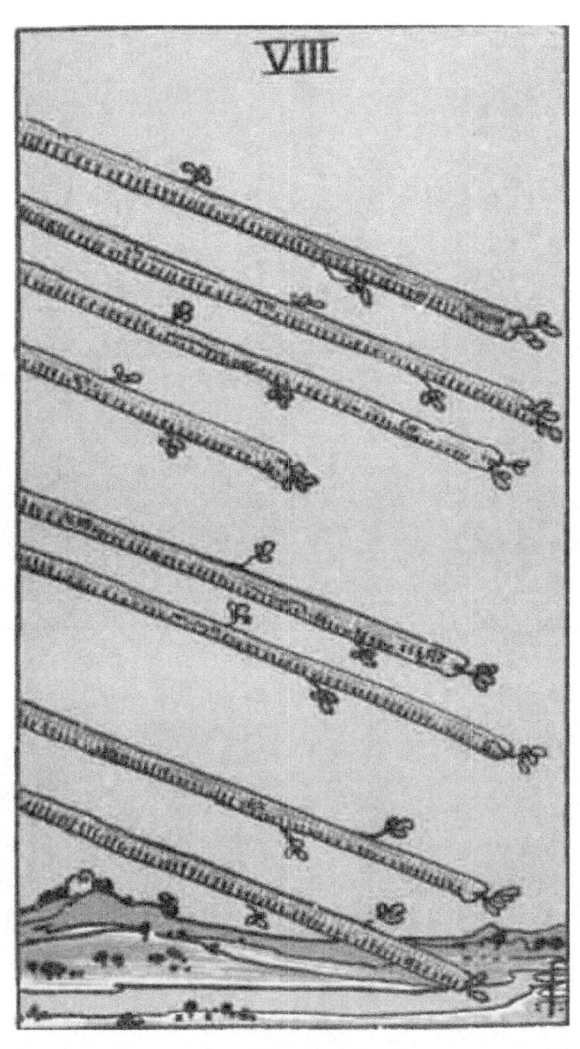

He comes across a man so worn
Nine wands there by his side
Though tired his perseverance
Show a resilience he can't hide

He sees a man with ten heavy wands
That makes him slightly bend
He is burdened now with battles won
But he got there in the end

The Fool's Journey with Cups

He has journeyed with a pentacle
A sword and with a wand
And now the fool must journey more
To see what lies beyond

Another magic hand appears
Holding a cup there up above
He understands this journey
Will teach emotions full of love

The Ace a new beginning
New relationship may be here
New love or strong emotion
A happy time so dear

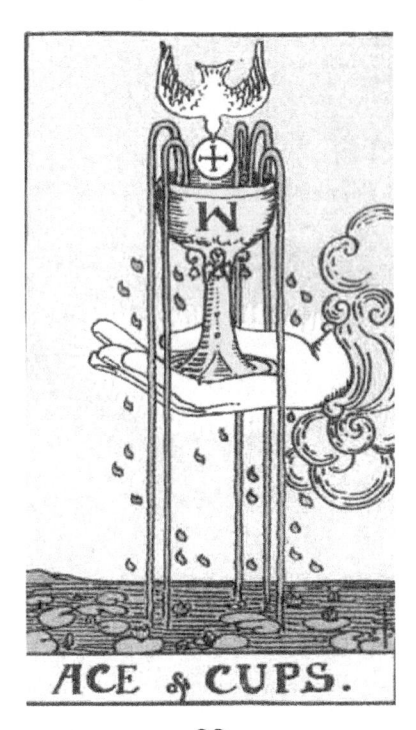

Two of cups two people
Lovers or sister and brother
Show mutual exchange of emotions
Between one human and another

He sees three maidens all a joy
Three cups they hold up high
A happy get together
Beneath a bright blue sky

He sees a man beneath a tree
In quiet contemplation
Three cups and one on offer
He sees them not in meditation

A man stands looking sad forlorn
Three fallen cups show troubled mind
With regret and sorrow he is unaware
Two upright cups stand there behind

Six of cups bring happy memories
Show the joys of children there
A lovely smiling sharing time
In this pretty village square

A man stands seven cups on high
Are they real or just illusion
He must decide what matters most
He is filled with much confusion

He sees a man walk slow away
Eight cups he leaves behind
Loneliness regrets and sorrow
He must move on to clear his mind

A man sits proudly smiling
Nine cups he shows with pride
Contentment satisfaction
Happiness he cannot hide

He comes across a happy place
Tens cups the ending of his quest
All wishes love and bliss are here
He knows emotion and is blessed

71

The Fool's Journey through the Court Cards

The Fool and the Royal House of Cups

The Fool then sees a castle
Sitting high up on a hill
The Royal House of Cups is there
Now he must journey still

He knocks upon the big wood door
Weathered now with years of age
Is greeted by a young man
It is the royal Page

Pray tell me sir what lessons
He asks the Page there at the door
I have quested far across this land
I am here to quest some more

I am a Page who carries messages
I am a creative idea knowing
Young inspirations come to me
Like the river always flowing

PAGE of CUPS.

He then sees a Knight a cup in hand
He sits on a big white horse
The Fool asks can you teach me more
The Knight says yes of course

Admire things of beauty
Be kind companionate too
Be charming and romantic
These things I say to you

He sees the Queen upon her throne
He is moved and bows so low
She is full of kind compassion
He asks what is it I should know

Show love and much compassion
Care for others when you can
Use the feelings deep inside your heart
And you will be a worthy man

QUEEN of CUPS.

Then he sees the King of Cups
Such a royal man is he
A sceptre there to show his power
And the fool bows with majesty

He learns a King is diplomatic
It is with kindness he does rule
Use all lessons here we teach
You will no longer be a Fool

The Fool and the Royal House of Swords

He had learnt about emotion
And now moved on towards
Another royal castle
The Royal Castle of the Swords

The royal Page of Swords
A young man sharp but kind
Exploring new ideas galore
About all things in his mind

The royal Knight however
Was a charger in his way
Ambitious dashing forward
It must be done without delay

The Queen of Swords upon her throne
Sat there with sword in hand
A gentle woman firm but fair
Direct but in command

The King of Swords so regal
With power and intellect did rule
Sharp of mind authority
These things he taught the Fool

The Fool and the Royal House of Pentacles

The Fool has learned emotion
How to control things in his mind
He sees the Castle Pentacles
Now what lesson will he find

He meets the Page of Pentacles
He is a bearer of good news
In business money goods and such
These things the fool could use

The Knight of Pentacles teaches him
How to work hard and achieve
Have routine and be consistent
Just be steady and believe

The Queen of Pentacles
A nurturing woman provider true
Charitable secure in worldly wealth
These things he can accrue

The King shows all abundance
Business leadership and more
With discipline and noble mind
You can achieve more than before

The Fool and the Royal House of Wands

He sees a castle up ahead
The royal banner with a wand
This royal palace calling him
And the Fool must now respond

The Page of Wands a young man
Full of energy and desires
Discovery with free spirit
These things the Fool admires

The Knight of Wands shows passion
He is ready for action here
Wand held high upon his horse
Go ahead no sign of fear

The Queen of Wands sunflower in hand
Vivacious passion strong
A wise cat sits in front of her
On her throne she does belong

The King of Wands a leader
Tells the Fool have a heart of fire
Vision honour drive and faith
You will achieve all you desire

KING of WANDS

The Fool's Journey End

Is this the Fool's journey end
Or is there more to learn
Must he go on travels new
Are there more badges yet to earn

He has journeyed through the majors
Through the minor cards he's been
Court cards showed him royal ways
So many things he's seen

He remembers the Magician
He met right at the start
Who showed him possibilities
Can be achieved all in his heart

He has come so very far
From those early days
Has changed from what he was before
In many many ways

He has journeyed long
And through so many lands
He has grown and loved and cried a lot
And now he understands

You journey far and live a life
You reach the end and then
You see a journey up ahead
And you set right out again

Printed in Great Britain
by Amazon